Welcoming the Stranger

Readying Ourselves for Christmas

Regent College Advent Reflections
Edited by Stacey Gleddiesmith

REGENT COLLEGE PUBLISHING
Vancouver, British Columbia

Published 2010 by Regent College Publishing
5800 University Boulevard, Vancouver, BC V6T 2E4 Canada
Web: www.regentpublishing.com
E-mail: info@regentpublishing.com

Regent College Publishing is an imprint of the Regent Bookstore
<www.regentbooksotre.com>. Views expressed in works published by Regent
College Publishing are those of the author and do not necessarily represent the
official position of Regent College <www.regent-college.edu>.

Library and Archives Canada Cataloguing in Publication

Welcoming the Stranger
edited by Stacey Gleddiesmith

ISBN 978-1-57383-452-0

1. Christmas–Meditations. 2. Advent–Meditations. I. Gleddiesmith, Stacey, 1975-

BV40.l66 2010   242'.33

contents

Our Response

God Prepares Us Room

Prepare Him Room

Acknowledgments

This project, touched as it was by many willing hands, was somewhat of a challenge to pull together in a timely fashion. In order to do so, I have called upon the help of many individuals who deserve greater thanks than my few humble words on this page. I can only hope that the praise and appreciation they receive from family, friends, and others who will undoubtedly be blessed by this book will be adequate payment for the hours and passion that they have given to this project.

First of all, I would like to thank all those to whom I turned for quick opinions and wise decisions: Richard Thompson, Patti Towler, Eugene Peterson, Holly Rail, Janina Mobach, Rebecca Pousette, Amber Ballard, and Andrew Gleddiesmith. Without your help, I would feel a great deal more insecure about releasing this book to the public! Thank you for your reassurances, your encouragement, and your occasional wise contradiction, which helped to provide fresh vision after hours of staring at the computer.

I would also like to show my appreciation to those without whom this book would not have been possible. Thank you to Rob Clements of Regent Publishing for another smooth and uneventful transition from idea to book. To Dal Schindell for sharing one of his favourite works of art for the cover (what a beautiful portrayal of this book's theme), and for his consistent and firm advice on internal consistency. To Rosi Petkova, who has poured her time into margins and fonts, colour and placement, in order to achieve this effective and attractive layout and design. And to Bethany Murphy, who has done an absolutely phenomenal job as both copyeditor and proofreader—I could not have asked for a better partner in the task of editing.

Finally, thank you to the very fine group of writers—both faculty and alumni—who have poured time and sweat and heart into their words. It has been my great joy and privilege to work with you, and I have absolutely no doubt that your words will have tremendous impact on those who read this book. They have on me. Thank you for accepting the invitation to write; for taking the time to consider Scripture anew; for extending to us the welcome that you have found in Scripture; for helping us to understand how to respond with hospitality; and for assisting us to consider, once again, the mystery of the incarnation.

Stacey Gleddiesmith
Editor

Introduction

The word "hospitality" conjures up images of fire-side chats, of tables groaning with good food and surrounded with the smiling faces of family and friends. Or perhaps other images spring to mind: foot-long grocery lists, the harried humidity of a kitchen running at full capacity, the hum of a vacuum cleaner.

I love the bustle of guests in a house, but this past spring, for one reason or another, we had three solid months of guests. Lovely, wonderful, dear people. Easy houseguests. For three months straight.

It didn't take long for things to unravel. Homemade soups, roasts, and stir-frys were heavily supplemented with order-in pizza, canned soup, and store-bought barbequed chicken. Dishes piled up in the sink. Toothpaste marks accumulated on the bathroom counter. My husband and I began to air disagreements we would normally have kept private. In short, the show broke down and reality took over. However, as the months ticked by, my husband and I began to realize the unexpected blessing of welcoming people into our messy home—into our messy life.

This little book is about that kind of hospitality. What does it mean to welcome God into all that we are? Into the squalor of our own personal stable? It is a holy paradox that God has made us welcome, but still seeks a welcome from us.

This book is an invitation to explore God's hospitality, your own hospitality, through the pens of the Regent community. There are two readings each day, morning and evening, on a single Scripture passage. Read the Scripture and the morning reflection—allow the words you read to percolate during your day. Read the Scripture again in the evening, concluding your day with the evening reflection—allow the words you read to guide you into rest. Not every reflection deals specifically with the birth narrative of Christ. That's okay. Advent, according to its positioning in the church calendar, is a time of fasting and preparation for the celebration of Christ's birth. Take these readings as just that—time to consider God's hospitality, and prepare to welcome him anew this Christmas.

So, in this small book, we will embrace together the vast and persistent welcome that God did, does, and will offer to us. We will consider the responses of God's people throughout history. We will consider various responses to the Christ-child. We will consider our own response to this stranger who lived (lives) among us. And, as we move closer to Christ, may we begin to understand the extravagance of his hospitality, and increase our capacity to extend that hospitality to others.

Let us welcome Christ (who entered humanity, a stranger among us) into all our squalor—for it cannot be worse than the first place in which he lay his head. Let us welcome other strangers into our homes: our dishes piled on the counter, our petty arguments, our canned soup and greasy pizza, our toothpaste marks on the bathroom sink.

Come, let us welcome the stranger.

Stacey Gleddiesmith
Editor

Night's Lodging

Across the purple-patterned snow

laced with light of lantern-glow,

dappled with dark,

comes Christ, the Child born from the skies.

Those are stars that are his eyes.

His infant face is wise

seen by my candle-spark.

But is he cold from the wind's cold blow?

Where will he go?

I'll wrap him warm with love,

well as I'm able,

in my heart stable.

Luci Shaw
1971

Author
Writer in Residence
Regent College

Genesis 2:4–15

Afterwards

We have discovered these things afterwards: monocots, dicots, the anther and filament. We have carried on the work of naming: *pedicels, dianthus, salvia.* We have unearthed the layers: the petals of the *corolla,* and beneath them the *sepals,* and next the apical portion, and further in, the basal portion. We can recognize the panicle inflorescence of oats, Kentucky bluegrass, tall fescue, grain sorghum.

Yet, this garden, this *paradise* (from the Iranian *pairi-* "around" + *diz-* "to make, form") remains cliché in its familiarity. It has been co-opted by polarizing questions about the age of the earth, the belief in gender roles, or not. The word *paradise* has become a worn out file—unable to sharpen the nail.

Deeper down, we must know it as memory. It is the thin skim of cream, scalenes that never tighten, the brume of bdellium rising through the floorboards. It is what we know by its absence and by our longing.

See, there was this garden, filled with trees and shrubs that bore fruit with seeds that would regenerate, increase. And my forebears were asked to cultivate and keep it. The fruit was good to eat and beautiful to look at: grapes, dates, figs, melons. It was a place that fit and was fit for them. And it all hinged upon a relationship with *Elohay Kedem*—God of the Beginning.

And still he asks us, as the Host that he is, to feast on the abundance, to participate, and to respond.

> *Lord God—Triune Father, Son, and Holy Spirit:*
> *make yourself powerfully, beautifully strange to us.*
> *Make your Word, again, strange to us.*

O ther things have come after as well. Blight, drought, and aphids (or were they before?). And, of course, the other garden, *Gethsemene* (from the Aramaic *gath shemanim*, literally "oil-press"), where the goodness of the original garden was replaced by holy anguish. On this side, it is easy to imagine the difference between the world before and the world after.

And yet there is a twist. The holy anguish that God experiences on behalf of a broken creation is followed by a holy persistence. The Creator God is also the covenant-keeping Yahweh who uses his name to show how he relates to us: he is Yahweh-*Yireh* (provider), Yahweh-*M'kadesh* (sanctifier), and Yahweh Sabbaoth.

Yahweh Sabbaoth: *The Lord of Hosts*. The Lord who is able to enter into times of crisis with his people and meet their needs. The Lord *who* hosts is also the Lord *of* hosts. The Lord God is both the one who welcomes us to his abundant feast and the one who, in times of crisis, delivers us. How often we choose to only see him as one or the other: the God of abundance or the God of necessity. And how much we miss by doing so.

Lord God, make yourself wholly familiar to us.
Bind yourself to us, come close. Teach us to receive
your hospitality, your gentle, meek spirit,
your powerful, decisive spirit, your self-sacrificing spirit,
your self, you. We do not know except by your grace.
We cannot live except through your life.

Ruth Pszwaro (née Tank)

Administrator, MacLaurin Institute
Minneapolis, MN
Poetry Editor, Geez Magazine
Regent Alum (MCS 2006)

Psalm 23

Extending the Shepherd's Table

The Psalter is certainly one of the most hospitable books in the Bible. If the psalmist can express his questions, outrage, joy, gratitude, desperation, and awe, then maybe I am also invited to be truly honest with my God. What a hospitable God, indeed!

I prayed Psalm 23 with and for a youth from El Salvador. He was about to cross over to the US illegally in search of his mother, who had left him and his brother when they were young teenagers in order to send money home.

It is a dangerous trip. Drug lords and corrupt police officers patrol the roads in Mexico, armed militia "protect" the US border. When my friend was about to face such inhospitable situations, it seemed appropriate and necessary to pray with him: "The Lord is my shepherd."

My friend went through the valley of the shadow of death, but in the end was reunited with his mother. I can only imagine the feast his mother must have prepared for him.

It seems clear that the psalmist writes about the Shepherd because of his own experience of feeling threatened or endangered. He talks *about* the Shepherd because, in those desperate situations, he is able to talk *to* the Shepherd: "you are with me."

Our personal situations might hold despair, confusion, or even danger. Regardless of whether we carelessly wandered into them or were dragged, we are invited to talk to the Shepherd. It is this hospitality we are invited to enjoy; it is this hospitality we are invited to extend.

M y wife and I are missionaries in Buenos Aires, Argentina. Anybody who has had to leave their hometown will understand how important it is to make new friends and how difficult that can be. As newcomers, few things are more meaningful to us than being invited to eat with a local family. When we lack meaningful relationships or interactions, we often begin to question ourselves. Being invited to share a meal makes us feel like normal, likeable people again.

The image of a God who prepares a table for us is one of the most welcoming images of God in the Old Testament. No wonder this image is also present in one of Jesus' most daring parables about God's character: the parable in which a father prepares a table for his wholly undeserving son (Luke 15:11–32).

The table is set for all of us! None of us deserves to sit at the table, but the shepherding Father has made space for each one of us. Let us open our hearts to God's welcoming heart. And let us, in turn, extend that welcome. For there may be no better way to prepare our hearts for God's feast than to go to the streets and alleys of the town and bring in the poor, the crippled, the blind, and the lame to join us at the table. Let us extend the Shepherd's table.

Lord, our shepherd, you set a table for us—
even when we are in the midst of difficult circumstances.
Help us to extend your hospitality to those who are outcast and needy.

David Nacho

Global Field Staff
Canadian Baptist Ministries
Buenos Aires, Argentina
Regent Alum (MDiv 2004, ThM 2010)

Ezekiel 36:8–12

The Last Word

From the beginning, Yahweh's plan for creation has been one of enduring hospitality. Creation's privilege and purpose, its beauty and integrity, culminate in being a sanctuary—a dwelling that God chooses to share with his human image-bearers. From the first words *ex nihilo* to the final word of new creation, the promise of God is to "finish" this relational gift through the permanent union of heaven and earth.

Yahweh intended from the beginning that the fame of his name and the *shalom* of his presence would extend to all the earth through his people and their land—offering divine hospitality through their relational unity. Tragically, Ezekiel testifies to the dissolution of this union, as Yahweh's people reject him and their holy calling. The surrounding nations misread the exile of these broken image-bearers, and the land's ensuing desolation, as Yahweh's impotence—instead of his consuming judgment over the adopted son who has denied his father and squandered the inheritance of Yahweh's blessing that is for the whole earth.

Judgment, however, is not Yahweh's last word. Yahweh's last word echoes his first words of life. This generous word of new creation is spoken first to the land: "Son of man, prophesy to the mountains of Israel" (v. 1); "I am concerned for you and will look on you with favour" (v. 9); you will produce fruit for my people.

Creation will not be abandoned or left to decay. Its destiny will be fulfilled as the habitation of God and his children, sharing in their revealed glory, and flourishing under the care of these new heirs of God.

During the exile of the adopted son, Israel, there is neither a kingdom of priests nor a land fit to mediate God's blessing to all peoples on the face of the earth. "What I have given them," says Yahweh, "will be taken from them"(Jer. 8:13). Even his divine presence departs from their midst (Ezek. 10).

And yet, the Lord is generous beyond measure. To the desolate mountains, hills, valleys, ravines, and empty towns left in ruin, the Sovereign Lord says: "I will increase the number of people and animals living on you, and they will be fruitful and become numerous" (v. 11)—more prosperous than before. The promise God made to Adam and again to Abraham, in union with the land, will be kept: "you ... will produce branches and fruit for my people Israel, for *they will soon come home*" (v. 8, emphasise mine).

With their homecoming comes rebuilding, planting, and herding—all attributed to Yahweh, who speaks and acts for the sake of his holy name. Chaos will again become like Eden, as God, people, and place are restored to permanent, lavish union. Out of the dry bones of death a people will live again. And a shepherd king of David's line—bone of our bone, flesh of our flesh, death of our death, and firstborn of a new immortal race—will lead his image-bearers home.

The Word who first spoke creation into being has become the last word and destiny of his new creation.

Cherith Fee Nordling

Sessional Lecturer, Theology
Regent College
Regent Alum (MCS 1997)

Psalm 84

Pilgrimage of Unexpected Happiness

This morning we are setting out to continue a pilgrimage. Sometimes we forget that. The humdrum routines of our day-to-day lives take over. Painful experiences that impress themselves on us make us lose sight of where we're heading. Selfish diversions cause us to dally rather than travel. The psalmist wants to impress on us the importance of focusing our undivided attention on the journey ahead.

"Happy," he says in verse 5, are those "who have set their hearts on pilgrimage" (my translation). It's a remarkable comment. Happiness, we would think, lies in reaching the destination, not in the travelling. And indeed the journey does have a purpose, a destination. It is a pilgrimage to the temple. The entire psalm is an expression of longing for the end of the journey. And the next five psalms also express the desire for union with the God who lives in Zion—but the psalmist hasn't arrived there yet. In the centre part of this psalm (vv. 5–7), therefore, he focuses on the journey itself. Happiness, he tells us, is ours even on the pilgrimage itself.

How can the psalmist say this? The hospitality of a God who turns the dry Valley of Baca into a place of springs and makes autumn rains cover it with pools has something to do with it. The more fundamental reason, however, is that God gives strength for the journey—he is our host, even within ourselves. True, we are longing for home—God's presence in the temple itself. But we also have a happy *pilgrimage*—if our heart is set on it.

The pain felt by the psalmist is all too real. "My soul yearns, even faints, for the courts of the Lord; my heart and my flesh cry out for the living God." Absence from the temple—absence from God—is simply insufferable. Every fibre of our being—"soul," "heart," and even "flesh"—cries out for the living God. Sometimes we suppress this deep-seated desire, but it returns with greater strength than before. What are we to do with this excruciating sense of the absence of God?

Perhaps we get a clue in the fact that so many people love this psalm. At least one reason for this is that they recognize that God is at home in the psalm. "How lovely is your dwelling place, Lord Almighty!" That is something we can say not just about the temple, not just about heaven, but also about the psalm itself. God has made the psalm his dwelling place.

This psalm, therefore, confronts us with a profound paradox. The very words that lament the absence of God render him present to us. Even in our moments of deepest darkness—when we seriously question how welcoming our God actually is—in the most unexpected ways, he is nonetheless present to us.

> *O come, Thou Key of David, come,*
> *And open wide our heavenly home;*
> *Make safe the way that leads on high,*
> *And close the path to misery.*
> *Rejoice! Rejoice!*
> *Emmanuel shall come to thee, O Israel.*

Hans Boersma

J.I. Packer Professor of Theology
Regent College

Exodus 3:1–4:17

Promises and Excuses

The season of Advent is a time of waiting, a good time to remember the promises of God given to Moses, and still kept today.

I have seen. "I have indeed seen the misery of my people" (3:7). God sees the struggles we face: the loss of a loved one, fear of the future, illness, pain. He sees the misery of the world: children in slavery, nations in crisis, the earth poisoned by human consumption. He has seen.

I have heard. "I have heard them crying" (3:7). God has heard our cries. It may feel at times that we are screaming at the void of God's presence, but God does, has, and will listen.

I have come. "I have come down to rescue them" (3:8). This is the great message of Advent—God comes to "seek and to save" (Luke 19:10). Christ has come and will come again to renew our broken and fallen world.

I am sending. "I am sending you" (3:10). While we live and wait in this season between Christ's comings, he is sending us to be agents of his kingdom, to be his image in this world.

Moses' response to this call is, "Who am I?" His first reaction is to say, "I don't think I'm the right person." But God responds with another promise: "*I will be with you*" (3:12). As God calls and sends us, he does not leave us to walk alone. The Spirit of God is ever present. He is "God with us."

When God speaks to Moses, Moses first replies, "Here I am." This phrase echoes throughout Scripture from the lips of those who hear and obey God. Abraham, Jacob, Samuel, and Isaiah all respond in this manner and go on to do what the Lord commands. Moses responds differently. He has seen a miracle, he has heard the voice of God, he has received the promises of God—but he responds with questions and excuses.

Moses first asks God how he should present him to the Israelites, essentially asking, "*Who are you?*"

He follows this with, "What if they won't believe me?" which springs from the deeper question of, "*Who am I?*" (3:11), or "What if they don't like me, won't listen to me, don't trust me?"

Drawing on this insecurity, he says apologetically, "I am slow of speech and tongue." "I'm not good at what you're asking me to do. I'm scared. *Why me?*"

Finally, Moses says what he has been leading up to all along. "*Please send someone else.*"

When I see the hand of God at work, do I ask, "Who are you?" or do I remember the God who keeps his promises? Am I choosing to question my value or remembering that I am chosen by God? Am I allowing God to speak through me or letting my fear consume me?

Too often we respond as Moses did. Yet, through all Moses' excuses, all our excuses, God is patient—reminding us of who he is, of who we are, and of who walks with us.

Renee Evashkevich

Worship Arts Faculty
Columbia Bible College
Abbotsford, BC
Regent Alum (MCS 2000)

Luke 1:5–25

God of the Humble—and the Not So Humble

Poor Zechariah. How many sermons have picked on him for his lack of faith, his lack of understanding, his lack of obedience in contrast to the splendid picture of humble, simple devotion we have in Mary a few verses later?

Zechariah the priest: the religious professional, the full-time holy man, confounded by a reality that he—of all people!—ought to have recognized, understood, and welcomed. He's standing right in the temple, offering incense. Didn't he expect God to show up? Why was he so astonished at the angel and his prophecy? Didn't he know his Bible? And why is he silenced for raising exactly the same sensible question raised by Father Abraham centuries before?

Well, you know how those theologians and clergy members are …

Yes, I do. It is an occupational hazard of all educated Christians to be so sure we understand the way things are that we assume that is how they must be—world without end. Zechariah would have known, of course, that angels did not routinely show up in the temple, and that there hadn't been a major prophet in Israel for four hundred years. His very expertise conditioned him against the unexpected—let alone the miraculous.

Today, let's stay alert to a surprise God might bring. Let's rejoice in what we have learned already, but may our grasp on that knowledge not become a rigid claw. Instead, may we keep our hands open to what God has yet to give us.

Zechariah the priest was silenced for his unbelief. But let's pay attention to what happens as the story continues beyond his mute gestures, as he emerges from the temple.

Despite Zechariah's doubts about God's promise, God keeps his word of blessing to him and to Elizabeth, and they are indeed blessed with a son: the great forerunner of Messiah himself, John the Baptist.

Moreover, while faithful Mary gets her magnificent song recorded later in this chapter, Zechariah is accorded the privilege of having his equally wonderful song come right afterward. It sounds themes in direct parallel with Mary's, just as his son would preach in concert with Mary's.

Advent is a time to recollect our failures, yes: our slownesses and stupidities and selfishnesses and sins of every other kind. But it is also the time to recollect the promise of God that our disobedient hearts can indeed be made righteous (v. 17), our darkness can be illuminated, our slavery ended, and our new life begun.

Our failures do not finally frustrate the powerful goodness of God. We deserve to be silenced forever, but instead God gives us a new song to sing—forever. So if we have been blessed with the gift of Mary's faith, let us sing with her. But I thank God that those of us who are more like Zechariah can also be welcomed into the Advent choir!

John G. Stackhouse, Jr.
Sangwoo Youtong Chee Professor of Theology and Culture
Regent College

Matthew 2

Who Will Welcome the King?

Herod had it made. After thirty years as king of Judea he had Rome's approval, and his wealth was growing as Judea grew more prosperous. But all this came at a cost. Herod had kept his throne by killing nearly everyone he thought might threaten his rule. Many of his good friends got the axe—so did his wife and two sons.

So, when visitors from the east came asking about a newborn king of the Jews, Herod knew what to do. The scholars he consulted told him about promises of a shepherd and ruler for Israel, and though Herod was ethnically half-Jewish and a convert to Judaism, these promises frightened him. Whatever sort of rule this strange king would bring, Herod considered it a direct threat to his power, wealth, and popularity. To stamp out this threat, he killed all the baby boys around Bethlehem.

For Herod, it didn't matter that this might be the greatest king yet, the King of kings who would finally bring peace. Herod had his own little slice of self-made peace and his own sham glory—and he was willing to do anything to hold onto it. Herod sensed that this strange king would unmake his rule.

Herod's self-protective measures horrify us—but how different are they from our own? How frequently do we choose our own hand-made kingdoms, our own peace—seeking to govern our own lives rather than accept the gracious rule of the King of kings? Will we reject or welcome his advent?

The strangers who arrived in Jerusalem hadn't read the prophets or consulted the religious authorities. They had read the stars. Some phenomena in the skies (perhaps conjunctions of Jupiter and Saturn in Pisces?) had tipped them off: a new king had been born to the Jews.

"Where is this king?" they asked. When their inquiries disturbed the priests, the scholars, and the king, the strangers looked up to the skies once again—and a star led them to the royal child and his mother.

As they arrived at the dwelling of the infant king, they jumped up and down; they whooped and cried tears of joy; they rushed into the house and threw themselves at the child's feet, offering him their most treasured goods. This is ecstasy—this is worship—this is a welcome fit for the King of kings.

While those who knew the Scriptures tried to kill the one Scripture proclaimed to be the King of kings, these foreigners from the east welcomed him. These pagans read what God published in the stars, the news that he was establishing a King over all the earth. In response, they set off on a great journey to pay homage to the new ruler. Overjoyed, they bowed before the King of the Jews and recognized him as their king too—as the Shepherd who would usher peace into the world. Let us do the same.

> So bring him incense, gold and myrrh,
> Come peasant, king to own him;
> The King of kings salvation brings,
> Let loving hearts enthrone him.

Robert W. Heimburger

Doctoral Candidate in Theology
University of Oxford
Regent Alum (MDiv 2008)

Matthew 16

Resistance and Relationship

How much of our talk about God, in his very presence, is equivalent to the wonderfully human discussion among the disciples in verse 7 when, in response to Jesus' caution about the "yeast" of the Pharisees, "they discussed this among themselves and said, 'It is because we didn't bring any bread.'" And how much of God's response to our talk about him is as exasperated as Jesus' response to the disciples in verse 11, "How is it you don't understand that I was not talking to you about bread?"

This inane discussion occurs within a passage containing enormous resistance to the truth about Jesus: about who he is, where he is headed, and, at an even deeper level, why his task is inescapable. The resistance of those who opposed Jesus is understandable; the resistance of those who followed him is embarrassing.

There is only one exception. The flash of insight Peter has: "You are the Messiah, the Son of the living God." Of course, Peter's insight only takes him so far—in the very next narrative he contradicts Jesus, as Jesus prepares his disciples for what is to come. Peter seems to think he can instruct "Messiah, the Son of the living God" on how he is to go about fulfilling the greatest and only hope of humanity.

The question that drifts out of this chapter, like a restless ghost, the question we ask ourselves as we wait for Christ's return, is this: are we more interested in discussing "who people say the Son of Man is" or in listening to the Word made flesh?

At the end of a meal a gracious Ethiopian guest will reassure the host by saying, "*Kfittfittu fitu yshalal*," which translates, "Your face is better than your food." Or, to draw out the meaning, "I didn't come to eat your food so much as to be with you." This phrase serves as a brief but poignant affirmation of what lies behind true hospitality: an invitation to relationship.

In Matthew 15 Jesus seizes the opportunity to host a multitude, and so in chapter 16 his references to bread and signs follow naturally from his act of miraculous hospitality. His guests let him down. They fix their minds on his food rather than his face. The disciples and the crowds have become focused on what Jesus can do for them, and have lost sight of who Jesus is.

The good host always offers his best, even though it may not be what we expect. The good guest accepts with gratitude that which is offered in love.

The ultimate act of hospitality is to make the guest a member of the family. At the end of chapter 16 Jesus offers this gift of familial belonging to his bewildered followers, but he does so with a grim reminder that, by accepting the best gift the host can offer, they make the fortunes and misfortunes of the host their own. Some demurred. Some still do.

At the end of this day, Lord Jesus,
did I come to eat your food,
or to be with you?

Steve Early

SIM Missionary
Adelaide, Australia
Regent Alum (DipCS 1990, MCS 2009)

Isaiah 1:1–20

An Invitation to Encounter

"My people have walked out on me," is how Eugene Peterson translates God's lament in this powerful opening chapter of the book of Isaiah (v. 4, *The Message*). He has been "forsaken," "spurned," as the TNIV puts it. We can feel the affront, the hurt, and, as the chapter unfolds, the outrage.

The context is eighth-century BC, when divided Israel is threatened by Assyria. God is angry with his people not only for turning their backs on him and the filial relationship he has nurtured (vv. 2–3), but because their behaviour has brought ruin (vv. 5–9). Such is the state of things that he rejects their sacrifices, yes, even their prayers—because they are meaningless without "understanding" (v. 3), without the relationship with God and neighbour that really matters.

In verse 18, the direction of the chapter changes. "'Come now, let us reason together,' says the Lord." However scholars may interpret the tone of these well-known words, God is extending an invitation—and it is all the more striking because of what has preceded it. The encounter itself is important, for both the Israelites and for us. It is where reparation can begin.

God wants to meet with us, no matter what has gone before. As we respond to his invitation to "Come," his longing is fulfilled, and "we learn to do right" (v. 17). What are our concerns this morning? Let us bring them to God in an encounter that will shape our day.

> *O come, Thou Day-Spring, come and cheer*
> *Our spirits by Thine advent here...*
> *And death's dark shadows put to flight.*

W hat is interesting about our passage, as we come to it again at the end of the day, is how unequivocal it is. It is clear that, besides neglecting God, the Israelites should have been prioritizing justice, which is something we too should prioritize: "Seek justice, encourage the oppressed" (v. 17). It is also clear that sin—rebellion and wrongdoing—is as distinct from a cleansed life as red is distinct from white (v. 18). It is clear that obedience leads to life; resistance, to death (vv. 19–20). We might note, in fact, just how much of the gospel is contained in this one Old Testament chapter.

When describing or evaluating things, we sometimes say they are "black and white." The gospel is unequivocal, black and white, but this clarity can be lost in the many shades of grey that characterize daily living.

This is how I often feel at the end of a day. When I start out, having spent time with God, I am clear about my path. As I look back, I see distractions and failures and am frustrated by the "shades of grey" that linger. What then?

It is good to remind ourselves that our God is constant. Ever hospitable, he is always inviting us to his table to "reason together," to find forgiveness, to satisfy our hunger. Returning to him we claim clarity again, entrusting ourselves to his care for the night and for a new day.

Rejoice! Rejoice! Emmanuel
Shall come to thee, O Israel.

Carolyn Scriven (née Armitage)

Editorial Consultant
Trustee, Friends of Regent College Canada Trust
Regent Alum (DipCS 1988)

John 1:1–18

But to All Who Receive Him

"His own did not receive him" (v. 11). What pathos is embedded in those words. Jesus, the eternal Word, came to his own world, his own people, but his own neither knew nor received him (vv. 10–11). He was destined to be their Light and Glory, but they would have none of it. He wanted to show them Grace and Truth, but they cast him behind their back.

The story is told of a son whose father sacrificed everything to put him through college. The day came when the young man graduated from university with the highest honours. The father, having made the long journey for the graduation, could not afford the appropriate attire for the occasion. What to do? He went anyway, assured of his son's understanding. When identified as the father of the brilliant scholar, all applauded—all except the embarrassed son who, with the curt remark, "I do not know him," disowned his heartbroken father.

We get angry at a story like that. What callous son would do such a thing? What father could endure such heartbreak?

Would not the Heavenly Father feel equally heartbroken?

But verses 10–11 aren't the end of the story; there is also verse 12: "Yet to all who did receive him"—thank God, there were some—to them "he gave the right to become children of God." Even if verse 12 doesn't take the sting out of verses 10–11, the glory of becoming children of God is none the less for that.

> *Where meek souls will receive him still,*
> *The dear Christ enters in.*

"The law was given through Moses; grace and truth came through Jesus Christ" (v. 17). Are there any words more lovely than "grace" and "truth?" Deeply rooted in the soil of the Old Testament, these are the qualities especially associated with the character of Yahweh. Of course there was also the law—society cannot function without it—but behind the law stands the character of him who more than any other was marked by grace and truth.

And now the revelation of the awesome truth: those qualities find their ultimate embodiment in the eternal Word, Jesus, who "was with God in the beginning" (v. 2). As for the Father, of course no one has ever seen him (v. 18). But the Son, he who is so perfectly identified with the Father as to be pictured as dwelling in his "bosom," it is he who has made the Father known; in fact, as the Greek text has it, it is "God the only Son" who has *exegeted* the Father!

And what has he made known about the Father? Many things, no doubt—but none more important than that he is full of grace and truth. And as the Father, so the Son; as the Son, so the Father. In them, grace and truth have kissed each other—the same grace and truth that they extend to us today and always.

> *O holy Child of Bethlehem,*
> *Descend to us, we pray;*
> *Cast out our sin and enter in,*
> *Be born in us today ....*
> *O come to us, abide with us*
> *Our Lord Emmanuel.*

Sven Soderlund

Professor Emeritus
Regent College

23

Genesis 12:1–5

An Invitation into God's Story

M oving to a new place strips away everything familiar. We feel help-less. Suddenly we don't know where to buy groceries or which streets will take us across town. We have to start our lives over, build new friendships, and find a new favourite coffee shop. Though we're fully aware of everything we've left behind, we don't yet know what awaits us.

In Genesis 12, the LORD invites Abraham to leave behind everything he knows—his country, his people, his extended family. Actually, God *commands* him to leave them all behind. This divine welcome is a call to obedience, a call to step into a new story.

Abraham's willingness to journey to an unknown country, which God prom-ises to reveal *after* he leaves home, begins a new chapter in the story of God's people. Abraham doesn't know how the story will unfold. All he knows is the God who calls him.

From our vantage point, a few chapters further on in the story of God's people, we know even more about this God. As Abraham's descendents recalled the Red Sea parting and the shepherd boy felling the giant, so we recall stories of God's faithfulness in our own lives. As we step into anything unknown, any new day, we know that God awaits us there, and that this day is one more page in the story of his people.

> *Lord, grant us a long memory of your faithfulness*
> *that we might step into your divine welcome,*
> *into the rest of your story,*
> *with obedience.*

A braham set out for Canaan without knowing what would happen. But along with the call, God extended a promise that he would bless Abraham. Though he left his people and his father's household, Abraham carried with him the promise that he himself would become a great nation.

What exactly does this blessing mean? Abraham wonders over the years. As year after year goes by and the promise is still not fulfilled, his faith falters. He jeopardizes the family line by offering Sarah to kings in self-protection, and jeopardizes it again by fathering a child through Hagar.

The ways of living Abraham had previously known are still more tangible to him than the blessings God brings or the unexpected way in which God works. Thankfully, God graciously takes Abraham's mistakes and folds them into his plan—the way an artist uses the limitations of wood or clay as part of her creation.

Despite his failings, Abraham's obedience results in blessing that spreads far beyond him. Incredibly, all people on earth are blessed through Abraham. His promised lineage extends all the way to Jesus, who finally extends God's welcome to every nation.

> *Lord, we are so weak, so often.*
> *We want to follow your path—but according to our own map.*
> *We want to obey—but only the commands that suit us.*
> *Give us the strength to obey your call into the unknown,*
> *whatever the cost,*
> *that we may continue to extend Christ's welcome to the world.*

Kristin Niehof

PhD Student
University of Oregon
Regent Alum (MCS 2010)

Isaiah 11:1-11

Vulnerable Hospitality

Vulnerability. This is not the word that comes to mind when we contemplate hospitality, especially God's hospitality. Most of the time we think hospitality should come from a place of power or strength—if only I had a nicer home, more space, better cooking skills, more to offer, and so on.

This passage, however, divulges to us something radically different about God's hospitality. God moves toward humanity, intertwined in a particular lineage: "A shoot will come up from the stump of Jesse" (v. 1). From our twenty-first-century Christian vantage point we know that this shoot is Jesus. But we tend to think of this "shoot of Jesse" as the adult Jesus, forgetting that he is also the baby Jesus who was born of a woman, in a stable. The God who comes to us in Jesus is dependent upon his mother and father for his well-being and survival. Moreover, his adopted family is displaced and homeless at the time of his birth. Thus, the host of our salvation starts his life as a dependent guest.

This reminds me of the old carol, "Lord, you were rich, beyond all splendour, yet for love's sake became so poor." God's hospitality begins in a place of weakness. It is in the surrendering of power and position that Jesus becomes the Saviour that we need.

> *Lo, how a rose e'er blooming, from tender stem hath sprung!*
> *From Jesse's lineage coming, as men of old have sung.*
> *It came, a floweret bright, amid the cold of winter*
> *When half spent was the night.*

"To show God's love aright, she bore to us a Saviour, when half spent was the night." As this old carol tells it, Mary gave birth to Jesus in the dark sleepy hours between night and dawn—the anxious and lonely hours in which our fears can overwhelm us and steal our sleep. Into this darkness the light of the world was made manifest in a tiny human being.

Jesus' parents must have been filled with uncertainty and trepidation. He was born at such an inconvenient time, right when they had to travel for the census. Imagine the pain and toil of birth in an unfamiliar place! "But Mary treasured up all these things and pondered them in her heart" (Luke 2:19). Did she know about Isaiah's prophecy? Did she know this was the one who would bring peace and harmony to the whole created order?

Isaiah tells us God's love will be shown "aright" through this person who became intertwined in the very fabric of humanity. The Spirit will rest upon him and he will judge with wisdom and understanding. This child will become a banner for all peoples, and the nations will be drawn to him. What a picture of hope for those dark, anxious hours. May you, like Mary, treasure up these promises and ponder them in your heart this night.

Isaiah 'twas foretold it, the Rose I have in mind.
With Mary we behold it, the Virgin mother kind.
To show God's love aright, she bore to us a Saviour
When half spent was the night.

Chelle Stearns

Assistant Professor of Theology
Mars Hill Graduate School
Seattle, WA
Regent Alum (MCS 1998)

Acts 11:1–18

Side-on Transformation

G od sometimes has to surprise us from side-on to transform our thinking—perhaps so we don't have our intellectual defences at the ready. He comes to us through story, poetry, music, a movie, a painting, or a vision. At these times, our response is usually more visceral than cerebral; something shifts deep within us and we are opened up to new ways of thinking and being.

After a mystical experience in prayer, Peter became more attuned to the mystery of God's presence in the world. His transformation was so profound that he was ready and willing to eat with those whom he had been taught to consider unclean and thus, in a way, to fear. He was opened up to embrace those who were "other" to his Jewish heritage and identity.

Both in his vision, and as he witnessed the Spirit descend on Gentile believers, Peter was surprised by God in a transformative way. He had to let go of his fears and mindset in order to see and participate in this new extension of God's hospitality. Peter had to trust God's invitation to act contrary to everything he had been brought up to know.

At times, we too are invited to relinquish our version of "truth" in order to grasp a greater Truth. Like Peter, we may need God's gentle and generous thrice repetition before we trust in God's mysterious, transformative revelation—from which we emerge saying, "Who was I to think that I could stand in God's way?" (v. 17).

The law-abiding Judaizers who accosted Peter in Jerusalem considered themselves gatekeepers, protecting their community from contamination. To them, Peter was guilty by association with the Gentiles.

At times, we too can fear difference—perceiving it as a threat to our community, rather than something that can enrich it. In doing so, we expend ourselves on "them-and-us" thinking, judging who is in or out, right or wrong. Our tendency is to marginalize the "other" rather than to extend God's persistent welcome.

Maybe we define the "other" as people from different races, places, or socioeconomic backgrounds. Perhaps we respond negatively to people with different skin colour, traditions, educational levels, or marital status; or to people with divergent views on politics, theology, gender, or sexuality. However we define the "other," whatever people we lump into that category, the reality is that they, just like us, are broken people needing to hear God's good news.

The good news was spread to the Caesarean household through Peter—and he, in turn, was transformed by what he saw: God's blessing granted to the Gentiles. It took inspired courage for Peter to enter into the story of Cornelius the centurion. But in doing so, he participated in God's bigger Story.

We too can be courageous in relinquishing fears and "them-and-us" thinking in order to enter into the story of our "Gentiles" and sit at the table with them. Perhaps, as we extend God's welcome in this way, we too will be transformed as we witness God's blessing.

In whose story is God inviting you to participate?

Vicki S. Leo

Architect
Melbourne, Australia
Regent Alum (MCS 2003)

Romans 3:21–26

Unconditional Welcome

My wife and I have a favourite tea house in Hay-on-Wye, Wales. While the tea and scones—with the necessary clotted cream and jam—are appetizing, it's not the food that provides the main appeal. Rather, it is the persistence of the hospitality, embodied in an incident that occurred this past summer.

We watched as a group of three came in, one of whom was a disabled woman in her forties. All three were welcomed by our friendly host and escorted to their table. When it came to ordering food, two of them expressed themselves clearly and understandably, but the third flapped her hands and uttered indecipherable grunts. She marched briskly to a glass cabinet on the other side of the room and pointed to a waxed "tart" with bright pink and white icing. Although not a real food item, this was what the woman wanted.

Our host, instead of responding negatively to the absurdity of the request, gently explained that the item was not for sale, made other suggestions, and eventually brought the woman a piece of coffee and walnut cake. All too often the disabled are rejected, but in this tea house, this woman was welcomed with a gentle persistence.

During Advent, it is instructive to remind ourselves of God's persistent welcome, in spite of the fact that we may be disabled, a Gentile, a slave, a woman, a child, marginalized, or poor. And, most poignantly of all, in spite of the fact that we are all sinners.

Why is the incident in the tea house so noteworthy? Normally welcome and acceptance are achieved by what we do and how we perform—if we fall short, we can expect to be rejected. Intuitively, we all understand that we usually get what others think we deserve.

That is why the first two words in the Romans passage are so important. "But now." Paul has made it clear that no one is justified by legal obedience to the law, since all fall short. In Philippians 3:9 Paul refers to it as "not having a righteousness of my own that comes from the law." Using the law as a standard for acceptance led all too easily to putting confidence in the flesh and seeking to develop a humanly centred form of righteousness. But now.

But now a different gospel has been revealed. While historically consistent with the Law and the Prophets, this new gospel is a righteousness that is from God—centred in Christ and bathed in grace. The entire trajectory is different. One invited us to work to achieve acceptance. The other argues that acceptance precedes anything we do. One was rooted in our vigilance and effort. The other flows from the character of God. One was based on a principle of apparent fairness. The other is grounded in a clear understanding of justice and justification.

My disabled friend in the tea house received a persistent welcome in spite of her limitations—and because of the character of our hosts.

Rod Wilson
President
Regent College

Luke 1:59–80

How Silently

Zechariah had nine months of silence to think about God's revelation to him. Quietly, he stood beside Elizabeth through her pregnancy, watching the growth of what he had told the angel Gabriel was "impossible." What a failure he must have felt—and yet here was God, blessing him still.

Proverbs 21:8 suggests we are known by our actions.

Consider Zechariah at the circumcision of his little son, when he is asked what the boy's name will be. Would he name his son in the "tradition" of his family? Tradition was a powerful motivator in Israel, a truth captured by Joseph Stein in *Fiddler on the Roof*: "because of our tradition, everyone knows who he is and what God expects of him." Would Zechariah's actions obediently follow God, as his wife's did—going against tradition by declaring the boy's name to be John?

The timing of this event is important: Zechariah first had to trust God's plan; second had to make this radical choice of name—and *then* he was blessed and his speech was restored.

What about us? How strong is our trust in God? Do we store away in our hearts those gifts of God's revelation to us, to reflect upon and guide our actions? Do we remember those *insights* that made all the difference in our lives, or that *comfort* when things were so dark, or the *forgiveness* when we did not deserve it? These are the gifts of the Spirit—providing light where we have none. They are signs of God's continued welcome of us, despite our own mistakes and shortcomings.

Zechariah's song was helpful to those present at John's circumcision, and is helpful to us today. His song puts the startling new revelation God has given to him into the context of Israel's walk with God since Abraham. It does not seem so amazing to us now, but it was then. Zechariah gave those present the understanding that God's promises of long ago were now being fulfilled.

How helpful it is when someone connects the dots for us and gives meaning to the confusion within and around us. This is the work of the Holy Spirit. We know this because it brings light into darkness and softens our hearts in gratitude.

Listen to how the *Living Bible* portrays Zechariah's softened heart as he looks upon his son and explains his part in God's new plan: "And you my little son shall be called the prophet of the glorious God, for you will prepare the way for the Messiah."

To arrive at this amazing understanding, Zechariah probably needed nine months of quiet gestation as much as Elizabeth did! His story reminds us of how much we need quiet to make sense of God's walk with us. This quiet, in which God moves to inform and transform us, changes how we act and react toward all of life.

> *How silently how silently the wondrous gift is given.*
> *So God imparts to human hearts the wonders of His heaven.*
> *No ear may hear his coming, but in this world of sin*
> *Where meek souls will receive him still,*
> *The dear Christ enters in.*

Ellie Robson

Public Health Research (Retired)
Edmonton, Alberta
Regent Alum (DipCS 1972)

Luke 1:46–56

Lifting the Humble

M ary's triumphant declaration of God's character almost bursts off the page with celebration. The angel's visit must have left her confused—uncertain about who would believe her, who would accept such a miraculous event. So when her aunt greets her with a prophetic word of welcome, you can imagine her sense of relief. Mary's doubt and confusion suddenly dissolve in a moment of blinding joy: "My soul glorifies the Lord and my spirit rejoices in God my Saviour!" (vv. 46–47). In that moment, the last of Mary's doubts and fears fled, and finally her spirit was free to recognize the magnitude of the events occurring within and around within her.

Mary's joy in God's work is illuminating: profoundly, her relief at a sympathetic audience does not lead to a greater focus on herself, but instead to a declaration of the Lord's work in her life—as a reflection of his character and a continuation of his pattern of work in the world. She sees God's choice of her as part and parcel of his character to exalt the humble and bring low the prideful.

Mary's celebration teaches us a model of praise: free of fear, she is given insight beyond her own life. She sees beyond God's hospitable choice of herself, to his hospitable work in the world—setting her story within God's story. Today, as you sit with Mary in her new-found confidence, rejoicing that God is still "mindful of the humble state of his servant," consider your own story in light of God's character and work in the world—and offer it in praise to God.

This morning, we considered Mary's celebratory placement of her own story within the character of God and his work in the world. As the day ends, it is important to remind ourselves of the *consistency* of God's character. Mary acclaims God's mercy and powerful acts, but more than anything, her focus is on the topsy-turvy nature of God's reign: the powerful and prideful are brought low, while the humble and those with no expectations of glory are lifted up. The hungry eat while the rich leave empty-handed. And, through it all, God does not forget his promises to his people.

Throughout Scripture God defines himself as the one who cares for the widow and orphan, feeds the hungry, clothes the naked, and executes justice for the oppressed. This God always opposes the proud and brings down the mighty—but delivers the humble and remembers his faithful ones. While we may find ourselves surprised by individual acts of God, as Mary was when the angel announced she would bear a child, God's deeds always fit within this known and consistently welcoming character.

How comforting to his people to be able to rest assured, no matter what the circumstances, that our God sees the humble—no matter how forgotten they may be by the world—and works to rectify oppression. We should all test our hearts today, and every day, lest we become "proud in [our] inmost thoughts" (v. 51). Rather, let us seek to be humble servants of God, working with him for his just and merciful reign on earth.

Mariam Kamell

Postdoctoral Fellow, New Testament Studies
Regent College

Luke 1:46–49, John 20:19–23

Through Locked Doors

I t may seem an altogether strange notion to compare the experience Mary celebrates in the Magnificat with that of the disciples after the resurrection of Jesus. As I have researched the church's exegesis of this latter passage, however, I have found that the miraculous passing of the risen Lord through the locked doors behind which the fearful disciples cowered is often considered analogous to the entrance of God into the closed womb of the Virgin.

Gregory the Great compares the sudden appearance of Jesus through the closed doors with "that which issued before the eyes of people from the Virgin's womb at his birth." Similarly, Peter Chrysologus writes, "I ask you, why is it doubted that divinity, which is without limit, was able to penetrate the hidden confines of the sealed sanctuary of a virgin's body preserved with her integrity fully intact, when, after the Resurrection, divinity, having acquired the density of our body in the mystery of the Incarnation, goes in and out through locked doors, and by such evidence shows that he is the Author of all creation, to whom creation offers no obstruction, but is obedient in every way?"

The similarities between these two events are helpful, as we seek to live in light of the incarnate and risen Son. Both events display for us the persistent hospitality of God: in the incarnation, as God became fully human for us broken and rebellious humans; and in the resurrection, as fearful, grieving, unbelieving disciples were suddenly invaded by the Presence that transforms, and were empowered for incarnational, hospitable mission to the world.

These passages hold two further similarities that inform our faith and teach us something about the character of God. The first is the joy experienced. Mary "rejoices in God [her] Saviour" (Luke 1:47); the disciples were "overjoyed when they saw the Lord" (John 20:20).

The second similarity is that both parties were in a state of humility when Christ came to them. Mary speaks of the mindfulness of God toward "the humble state of his servant." She seems to have had a keen awareness of her unworthiness for the great privilege of bearing the Messiah. She is, after all, to become the *Theotokos*—the bearer of a Man who is God—to the world.

The disciples do not recognize their unworthiness in the same way. Instead, they have *been* humbled by various means: Peter by his denial, even more humiliating in light of his previous protestations; the rest by their forsaking of Jesus in his hour of deepest need. Some have suggested the disciples did not believe the women who had seen the Lord on Easter morning because they wondered why the women, and not they, were worthy of the first appearance of the resurrected Christ.

Graciously, Jesus does not wait long to reveal his risen-ness to these fearful, forlorn disciples. And by grace abounding, they, along with Mary, become participants in the sent-ness of the triune God to the world. Graciously, Jesus does not wait long to reveal himself to us, in our humble state—but by grace abounding makes us, in turn, bearers of his welcome to the world. May we receive him with joy.

Ross Hastings

Associate Professor of Pastoral Theology
Regent College

Luke 4:14–21

A Lucan Examen

Most of our days begin with the ordinary, rather than the unexpected. Just as well, since most of us prefer routine to surprise.

So it is with our morning devotional exercises. We spend time in friendship with God. We reflect on Scripture. We pray. And, having been reassured and comforted, we enter into the fray of a new day.

The Sabbath day in Nazareth also began as usual. There was nothing abnormal about Jesus, the son of Joseph, son of Heli (3:23), reading the Scriptures (4:16). And while those in the synagogue were attentive (4:20), likely nothing much was expected. Jesus' baptism and temptation had taken place elsewhere (4:1), and even though reports about Jesus were circulating in Galilee (4:14), it was business as usual in Nazareth (4:16).

But in the midst of the ordinary came surprise: the assertion that this Scripture was being fulfilled in the here and now (4:21). And even more startling was the idea that this song of the Messiah was centred on their home-grown boy. This son of Joseph was announcing that Yahweh's full deliverance and healing would come to them through him (4:22). Clearly, this rocked the boat of normal expectations.

For those of us familiar with the routines of piety, what are we not hearing and seeing in God's way with us? To what song are we tone deaf? Have we already made up our minds about how God should work and who God should use?

The challenge for the faithful is always the challenge to a greater receptivity.

At day's end lies the gracious invitation to come into God's presence before we go to sleep. That welcome invites us to give thanks for the blessings of the day, to seek forgiveness for our failures and faults, and to seek God's renewing strength for the new day that awaits us.

In this Lucan examen (Luke 4:14–21) we are invited to give thanks for the way the Spirit was with us during our day, giving empowerment and wisdom. We give thanks for the healing and freedom Christ has brought to our lives, and we rejoice in the insights and discernment we have been given—through the gospel and Christ's presence with us.

But there was more to our day than sheer goodness. We also want to acknowledge there are areas of poverty, blindness, and bondage in our lives. And some of those things were also evident in our day.

For these things, O Lord, we are truly sorry. We have much growing up to do. A fullness of life in Christ through the Spirit beckons us. So Lord, please help us in this journey toward you. Since Christ came to bring forgiveness, freedom, healing, and deliverance for all, and particularly for the poor (4:18), help me, Lord, beyond my self-preoccupation and selfishness. Give me a heart for you, for your kingdom, and for your strange, up-side-down way in the world. And so, give me your hospitable heart for the poor, that they may find the Christ of healing and hope.

Charles Ringma

Professor Emeritus
Regent College

Genesis 18:1–8

Entertaining Angels

A braham's welcoming of the three visitors has long been seen as an expression of Middle Eastern hospitality. Desert travel, always risky, is protected by the venerable practice of welcoming the stranger. In my tent, you are under my protection. Genesis 18 is different only because the visit, and the visitor(s), come from heaven. We might call it the First Great Advent.

The text begins with God ("the LORD"), not Abraham. Three persons appear before the patriarch, but from the beginning it is a visit from "the One." Although the Trinity is not mentioned explicitly, the text is clear. The "three men," who speak and are sometimes addressed in the singular, in some mysterious way can be characterized as "the LORD" (v. 1).

From at least the fourth century, Christian art produced a variety of visual representations of this scene—overcoming a Jewish reluctance to picture God, while struggling with the tension of unity in diversity. But the key is not the travellers' appearance, but their presence. God, the divine LORD, has broken the silence of heaven, accepted the risk of travel in a hostile land, and stands before Abraham at the door of his tent.

Whatever can be said about the "three in one," Abraham (and Sarah)—no less than Mary (and Joseph)—experience what happens when God comes down to earth. As we approach Advent, in the midst of our own day and age, can we expect a God who comes down to meet us today—where we are?

The corollary to the LORD's appearance is Abraham's welcome. As the writer of Hebrews reminds us, it is possible to "entertain angels unawares," making it doubly important to "entertain strangers" (13:2 KJV). Abraham is the model.

If it was risky for the LORD to wander through the desert, it was also risky for Abraham to welcome three strangers. Did something tip him off to this being no ordinary visit? What did they look like? How were they travelling? Were there signs of divinity?

In a fifth-century mosaic in Rome's Santa Maria Maggiore, the three visitors are pictured twice: in the top panel being welcomed by their host; and below, seated at a table. Halos surround all three, but in the first instance the centre figure has a full-body halo (*mandorla*), perhaps reflecting his special role as the incarnate Son (see Justin Martyr). A century later, in Ravenna's San Vitale church, the visitors are portrayed as carbon copies of one-another (God's unity)—appearing within a context where Abraham's festal offering is nothing short of a Eucharist.

How, then, do we welcome the Triune God when he comes—whether to Abraham in the heat of the day, or to Mary as a babe in the womb? Or, with the early Christians, as we break the bread? And, above all, when he comes as the ever-present Spirit while we go about our daily tasks?

Hebrews sums it up: "Do not forget to show hospitality ... " (TNIV). Seeing God in the stranger, the alien, the widow, and the orphan, ensures that we won't miss him when he comes.

Carl E. Armerding

Founding Faculty Member
Former President
Regent College

Genesis 28:10–22

You Will Be My God

J acob was the consummate deal-maker—a man of action—always on the lookout for opportunities and advantages. And, like many blessed with shrewdness, he was tempted to use his skill to his own advantage. (His schemes to defraud his elder brother Esau of his birthright and his father's blessing are infamous.) But I imagine Jacob as also possessing the best qualities of an entrepreneur, as a guy who could see possibilities where others saw none.

Coming into relationship with God can be a particular challenge for such people. After all, what can one bring to the negotiation table when dealing with the Master of the Universe?

And yet, that is how Jacob responds to his extraordinary dream. While the text says he made a vow, it appears to be more of an attempted negotiation. "Okay, God," Jacob seems to say, "you stay with me and give me all the food and supplies I need on this journey, and in return you will be my God and I will give you a tenth of all I have. Is it a deal?"

I imagine God may have chuckled at the childishness of Jacob's attempt to negotiate with him. And yet he accepted Jacob as he was—drawing him closer and closer, as we see throughout the remainder of the book of Genesis.

In light of the immeasurable greatness of God, Jacob's attempt to strike a deal with him seems almost pathetic. Yet the God of grace will use those very qualities—Jacob's shrewdness and deal-making skills—to establish and protect the nation Israel.

J acob has yet to enter the proverbial school of hard knocks in our passage. He is a young man, full of confidence, drive, and even hubris. (Who in their right mind would attempt to make a deal with Yahweh!) His faith is embryonic, not yet seasoned and matured through the vicissitudes of life. But here is where it starts, here is where we see a fundamental, if tentative, shift in the young man's heart.

In the previous chapter, when speaking to his father, Jacob refers to Yahweh as "the Lord *your* God." In today's reading, he responds to God's call through the dream by vowing that (if God goes with him and provides for him) "the Lord will be *my* God." What a difference a simple possessive adjective can make! "My father and grandfather's God shall be *my* God." How the angels must have rejoiced.

Here is the beginning of a welcome, the beginning of an acknowledgement of dependence on God—the first tentative steps of a self-reliant, talented man toward relationship with God. Here is the beginning of Jacob *owning* the faith he received from his forefathers.

Surely this is one of the great challenges for all God's people—to own our faith. Whether raised by Christian parents or not, we are all tempted to be content with a derivative relationship with God. For each individual, the call of God remains consistent: "I will be *your* God."

Jesus, may my welcome of you this Advent be personal and unreserved,
my relationship with you direct and intimate.

M. Patti Towler

Vice President (External)
Legal Counsel
Regent College
Regent Alum (DipCS 1996)

Matthew 1:18–25

Fostering the Messiah

Matthew does not give us extensive details of the annunciation, the pregnancy, and Jesus' birth. Instead, Matthew introduces Jesus by means of a genealogy (1:1–17), identifying him as the Messiah (*Christos* "the Anointed One"), the son of David, the son of Abraham.

We are told that Mary the mother of Jesus was engaged to a man named Joseph, but before the marriage had been consummated "she was found to be pregnant through the Holy Spirit" (v. 18).

Whatever knowledge Mary had about the nature of the child in her womb, it had not yet been revealed to Joseph. How did Mary find the courage to tell him about her pregnancy?

Joseph, of course, concluded that this pregnancy had occurred in the usual manner; as far as he knew, Mary had been unfaithful. This presented him with a dilemma. The engagement represented a permanent commitment, the first stage of life as a married couple; to break off the relationship required a formal divorce. If Joseph divorced Mary publicly, she would be subject to a disgrace that would be with her the rest of her life—zealots in the community might even stone her. "Being a righteous man," Joseph chooses to divorce her quietly without calling the matter to public attention.

From a human perspective, that could have been the end of the story. But God had prepared a place for the Messiah to enter the world, and that place included a foster father, a righteous man who would provide a home in which Jesus would grow up to extend hospitality to the world.

Before Joseph could implement his plan, "an angel of the Lord appeared to him in a dream," encouraged him to take Mary as his wife (v. 20), and revealed to Joseph that the child had been conceived by the Holy Spirit— and his name was to be "Jesus" (*Yeshua* "Yahweh saves").

The birth of this child was not only confirmed by angels, but also foretold by Scripture (Isa. 7:14), a recurring theme of Matthew's gospel. Jesus, the One who saves, is also "Emmanuel" ("God is with us"). The name "Jesus" indicates what he does. "Emmanuel" reveals who he is.

"When Joseph awoke from sleep, he did as the angel of the Lord commanded him" (v. 24). Joseph represents the faithful disciple of Jesus—desirous of following the Lord and doing what is right, but also open to illumination.

Reading through the rest of the New Testament, we have the impression that Joseph was no longer alive to participate in the drama of Jesus' public ministry. But we can be sure that Joseph the carpenter proved a faithful foster father as well as a true son of Abraham.

And what does this means for us, at the conclusion of a busy day? We may not be faced, as Joseph was, with such an extraordinary circumstance—but we are asked, as Joseph was, to seek righteousness in our daily actions. And not only to seek righteousness, but to be open to the miraculous intervention of God as we, too, seek to make a home for the Messiah and to extend his hospitality to the world.

W. Ward Gasque

Founding Faculty Member
Professor Emeritus, E. Marshall Sheppard Chair of Biblical Studies
Regent College

Luke 1:26–38

Posture of Reception

The angel Gabriel addresses Mary mysteriously: "Greetings, you who are highly favoured! The Lord is with you." Mary's first reaction is to be "greatly troubled," but the angel quickly calms her fears: "Do not be afraid, Mary, you have found favour with God." Gabriel brings a world-shaking public announcement, but at the same time engages Mary in a highly personal encounter.

Fra Angelico, a Dominican monk, painted a number of Annunciations on the walls of the San Marco Convent in Florence. On the stairs to the dormitories is a fresco that imagines Gabriel and Mary in conversation in the cloistered garden of the convent. Gabriel, full of energy, announces the coming of the "Son of the Most High" to a humble, awestruck Mary, seated on her simple stool. The Lord God will give her son, Jesus, the throne of David. He will reign over the house of Jacob forever.

This grand Annunciation in a public space may be contrasted with a second, humbler fresco in Cell 3 (possibly Fra Angelico's own room). Here Gabriel and Mary are pictured in intimate conversation about the mysterious news. St. Dominic the preacher prays silently as the angel speaks: "Do not be afraid, you have found favour with God."

These two paintings tell two parts of the story: God's concern for a humble young woman, and the joyful proclamation of a new kingdom. In both, Mary is portrayed in a posture of reception—of the angel who is a stranger, and of this strange news, that through her womb God will bid the world to make his Son welcome.

When she receives the words of Gabriel, Mary asks an entirely rational question: "How will this be, since I am a virgin?" She is told that the Holy Spirit's presence and power will overshadow her, and that her older relative Elizabeth is also miraculously with child—a sign that nothing is impossible with God. To a young, frightened teenager, both of these answers must have seemed strange.

A third Annunciation by Fra Angelico in the Prado Museum shows how Mary responded to these challenges. On the left side, an angel powerfully expels Adam and Eve from the beautiful Garden of Eden. Mary is in precious lapis blue on the right, and Gabriel is portrayed in the centre. Diagonally across the panel is a solid gold band issuing from God's hand, containing a white dove.

While many earlier Annunciations portray the overshadowing with a heavy dark line of text issuing from Gabriel's mouth, here it is portrayed with the purest of light and reflections of precious gold. This divine overshadowing moves across the lapis blue of Eden's sky, across an arched canopy of stars, to fall on Mary's crossed hands and heart. It contains no words but is filled with the power of the Most High God.

Mary leans receptively forward and seems already to cradle the new life within her. The painting suggests that Mary responded with openness and humility because, in that moment, she experienced God's power. She knew intimately that nothing is impossible with God.

"I am the Lord's servant. May it be to me according to your word."

Lindsay Farrell

Head of the School of Arts and Sciences
Australian Catholic University
Brisbane, Australia
Regent Alum (MCS 1993)

Luke 2:8-20

The First Welcome

Most mornings when I drive my half-hour trip to work, I thank God for the fresh new day he has provided for me. I pray he will watch over my family, and for the day ahead. I bring him certain issues that are on my mind.

What were the shepherds' prayers as their new day broke? Something had happened to them a few hours earlier that changed the course of their lives. *"Today* in the town of David a Saviour has been born to you; he is Christ the Lord" (v. 11). Rough, stinking, uncouth, uneducated, ill-mannered—they alone had been invited by a host of angels to meet the long-awaited King, the Saviour, the Messiah.

And how would they know him—they who were so unfamiliar with class, royalty, fine buildings, and dazzling decor? God's plan included a sign these humble shepherds would recognize better than anyone else. "You will find the baby … in a manger" (v. 12). A manger!

They saw him, they adored him, and they raced home to share the news that this tiny wrinkled child was the King they had anticipated, the Saviour for whom they had longed. And they, because of that unforgettable angelic invitation, were his first visitors—his first guests.

> *Shepherds, why this Jubilee?*
> *Why your joyous strains prolong?*
> *What the gladsome tidings be*
> *Which inspire your heavenly song?*

H e knew his life was over.

It had been a night like any other: a couple of lambs birthed, the flock moved to fresh grazing, meat and rough wine for dinner, rest by the fire after the long day. It was a dark night, stars shining in the clear desert sky—and then—was it the music that woke him? Was it the singing? Or was it the light? Startled out of sleep, his mind alert, sharp, and ... *terrified*. He knew his life was over.

He was nothing more than a lowly shepherd: the grandson of a shepherd, the son of a shepherd, the father of a shepherd. He could not speak. He could not move. Fear bristled through him: raw, stark, fear; fear he had never known before. He knew his life was over.

How could a voice be so powerful and strong, yet so gentle and warm? "Do not be afraid." Only then was he able to truly hear the music, to see clearly the glorious light, the holy beings whose joy was almost palpable. And peace, unlike anything he had ever experienced, washed over every cell in his body. He was no longer afraid. But still—he knew his life was over.

He bowed his head. He waited for the end—but then the voice told him what he must do. And he knew, in an instant, that his life was about to begin.

> *Come to Bethlehem and see*
> *Him whose birth the angels sing;*
> *Come, adore on bended knee*
> *Christ, the Lord,*
> *the newborn King.*

Kit Schindell

Director, Patient Relations
Providence Health Care
Vancouver, BC
Regent Alum (DipCS 1972)

Luke 2:25–35

Embracing the Child

"My eyes have seen your salvation" (v. 30). What did Simeon actually see? An ordinary occurrence: a peasant couple arrives in the temple court with their newborn son. There was no heavenly sign, no halo around Jesus' head, no angel visitation to announce him to Simeon. There was nothing outwardly unusual about this baby that marked him as special (Isa. 53:2). Yet, when Simeon saw Jesus, he recognized the profound working of God in that helpless child.

The key to Simeon's penetration is in the opening sentences of this passage. We are given a picture of a man whose heart was deliberately tuned to the heart of his God. This devotion was accompanied by sensitivity to the movement of the Holy Spirit and an expectant faith (vv. 25–26). It was Simeon's sensitivity that led him to the temple for his divine appointment with the Messiah. It was his expectant faith that allowed him to go beyond outward sight to see the truth of what was happening that day in the temple. His life of devotion allowed him to faithfully carry out his appointed task—the great privilege of welcoming the child into the temple.

The work of God's salvation, seen in Jesus, is "prepared in the sight of all people" (v. 31). We too are called to see Jesus and his salvation. Let us, by the grace of God, make this our task today.

God grant us expectant faith and eyes enlightened by the Holy Spirit
that we might see the child
as he was, as he is, and as he shall be.

"Simeon took him in his arms" (v. 28). This was a pivotal action. Simeon received the child—took Jesus to himself. It was an expression of profound trust.

Simeon's prophecy regarded the conflict that would arise around Jesus (vv. 34–35). Jesus did not bring Israel relief from their very real external trouble: the foreign domination of Rome. Instead, Jesus dealt with the hearts of the people, revealing thoughts and motives. Even Mary was not exempt from the piercing of the Word of God incarnate (v. 35).

All this Simeon embraced. Seeing the child and knowing, through the power of the Holy Spirit, something of the strange life this child would lead, Simeon held Jesus to himself. How much of this prophecy did Simeon understand? We don't know. What is important is that Simeon embraced the fullness of the Messiah—both that which he understood and that which remained a mystery. Simeon's life of devotion led him to know God and, knowing him, to trust God with all he did not understand and would not witness. He counted the salvation of Israel complete in this weak and needy child.

The child continues his work today, by his Holy Spirit. We, too, are pierced—the poverty of our souls laid bare. This is done in mercy, that we might be enabled to receive Christ's infinite riches. Let us, like Simeon, embrace the fullness of this strange child and, in so doing, be at peace.

God grant us the strength to embrace the child
as he was, as he is, and as he shall be.

Kathryn Penner

Spruce Grove, Alberta
Regent Alum (DipCS 1992)

Isaiah 9:2–7

Welcome God's Light

"The people walking in darkness have seen a great light." In the first phrase of our text, the prophet summarizes the dark state of God's people—for Israel's stubborn unrighteousness has led finally to God's judgment: they are oppressed by Assyria and will be spiritually blind until their discipline has ended. Still, our hospitable God desires relationship with his people and longs for their repentance and salvation.

It is the fulfilment of this hope that Isaiah foretells, declaring not only Israel's restoration, but a future era of peace for all humankind. This will be inaugurated by the joyful coming of spiritual light and salvation, the birth of a son who will rule justly in the line of David. Both Matthew (4:12–16) and Luke (1:79) present Jesus as this light. Amidst shining divine glory, angels proclaim to humble shepherds news of peace and joy—the birth of a Son, a Saviour in David's line (Luke 2:8–14).

As we begin this day, Isaiah's promise is ours. Whatever darkness we experience, even if it is of our own making, our hope is in the Light which has come, the King who has been born, and the salvation which he daily offers. The response required of us is to make him welcome.

A time will come when night will be no more (Isa. 60:19–20), but already we rejoice, "for God, who said, 'Let light shine out of darkness,' made his light shine in our hearts to give us the light of the knowledge of the glory of God in the face of Christ" (2 Cor. 4:6).

Israel walked in darkness because the people refused to trust God's wise rule, looking instead to their own wisdom, to human resources, even to idols and divination—and so they became spiritually blind (Isa. 6:9–10). Isaiah foretells Light's coming and the healing of blindness with the arrival of a righteous king (Isa. 9:2–7; 32:1–8; cf. 42:6–7).

In John's Gospel, Jesus claims to be the light (John 9:5), healing a blind man and bringing him out of darkness not only physically, but spiritually. This man models for us the welcoming of God's light as he humbly trusts Jesus, not only as a prophet sent from God, but as one worthy of worship. At the same time, some of the Pharisees, trusting their own wisdom, arrogantly declare Jesus a sinner and reject their Messiah; their spiritual blindness is confirmed (John 9:41; 12:37–41).

At the end of this day, we welcome God's light and salvation afresh as we trust his son, our righteous king, "Wonderful Counsellor, Mighty God, Everlasting Father, and Prince of Peace" (v. 6). We trust Jesus with all that this day has held, with the night to come, and with all that tomorrow will bring. Even when his ways are hard, with open-hearted humility we trust his wise rule, acknowledging our blindness and receiving his healing. "Put your trust in the light," Jesus appeals (John 12:36; 46). "Arise, shine," calls the prophet, "for your light has come, and the glory of the Lord rises upon you" (Isa. 60:1).

Ruth Norris

PhD Student
Cambridge, UK
Regent Alum (MCS 2007)

Exodus 12:1–13, Luke 22:14–20

A Meal to Remember

What a meal to commemorate: blood on door posts, the sizzle of lamb roasting, the taste of bitter herbs sharp on tongues. Cloaks tucked up into belts, the rub of sandals on feet as families crouch by fires, meat crammed hurriedly into mouths.

This night, the LORD will pass over. He will come to bring judgment and deliverance, and blood will be the sign. Blood will cause the summons—making the word "Go!" echo through the still-dark night. Generations will celebrate this huddled, hurried meal that turned to dust in the Israelites' mouths with fear.

Have you ever thought it strange that God preceded his deliverance with instructions for a meal? That he played host before he played deliverer? This strange, hasty meal is a testament to God's love and care for his people. God not only delivers his people, but provides strength for their journey—for the suffering they are about to face.

"I have eagerly desired to eat this Passover with you before I suffer" (v. 15).

"We do not," says the author of Hebrews, "have a high priest who is unable to empathize with our weaknesses" (4:15). No, we have a high priest who is also the sacrifice, also the identifying blood on our doorposts. We have a high priest who, being fully human, required strength for the journey.

> *Lord, we remember your humanity this Advent.*
> *We remember your fragile body cradled by a manger,*
> *your need for food and drink.*
> *May we readily accept your provision for the journey.*

What a meal to commemorate: faces lit with joy at Jesus' expression of eagerness, eyes narrowed in sudden confusion—questions sharp on the tips of tongues.

Did this meal also turn to dust in the disciples' mouths, as they strove to understand these hard words? Did their eyes widen in frightened acknowledgement as they took the bread that was body?

This night, the LORD will be passed over to his enemies. He will come to bring grace and deliverance, and blood will be the sign. Blood will cause the summons—making the word "Go!" echo through the still-dark night. And generations will celebrate this quiet, revolutionary meal that turned to dust in the disciples' mouths with confusion. Generations will come to this table—will set a table for others.

For there is always strength for the journey—no matter how hasty, how confusing the meal. Bread moves through teeth, over the tongue, and down to our gut where it is churned into strong limbs and steady steps. Wine, held in the mouth and savoured, poured down the throat to rest in the belly, flows into eloquent lips and work-worn hands. What a simple reminder of God's deliverance, salvation, and daily provision: a meal. We remember three times a day, seven days a week.

And we have a high priest who not only partook of this meal, being fully human, but who also, as the fully divine host, provides this meal for us.

Lord, we remember your divinity this Advent.
We remember your provision for your disciples,
and for us.
May we joyfully extend the table you have set.

Stacey Gleddiesmith

Staff Writer
Regent College
Regent Alum (MDiv 2007)

John 13:30–14:4

Going Home

Every now and then, Jesus hinted that one day his disciples—that little band of chosen ones who, for three years, had followed him literally in his travels and metaphorically by learning from him the realities of kingdom life—would be left to manage without him. Evidently, however, they had not taken him seriously till this moment. But now Jesus was making them face up to his imminent departure, and it was hitting them like a bombshell. Having assumed all along that their master, whatever he might say in his black moods, was headed for some sort of national leadership, they were devastated.

Jesus, the infallible heart-reader, spoke at once to their condition, telling them they must not give way to their present grief and confusion. He was returning, he explained, to his Father's home, there to set up a permanent place of welcome for them.

Though he did not speak of it at this point, Jesus wanted them to realize that he would be clearing the path for them, and all believers like them, by his sin-bearing death and death-conquering resurrection. And he meant them to realize also that, foreseeing their deaths (as he was to show in Peter's case, 21:19), his coming back for them would be a personal meeting.

So that is what we, Jesus' twenty-first-century disciples, have to look forward to. Whenever and however we die, at the heart of the death-process will be this personal meeting, as Jesus comes to us to take us home. Thus we shall be brought into the reality of our hope of glory. What joy!

"I would love to spend time there. Do you know of a place to stay?" These words might be spoken in conversation anywhere. "Place to stay," of course, means *good* place to stay, where one can remain as long as one wishes and enjoy every moment of it. This particular use of "good" finds its apex in the Greek word *monê*, when Jesus uses it for "places to stay" in his Father's house.

His hearers' hearts, we learn, were "troubled," because he had said he was leaving. What would they do next? The many forms of the inner nightmare that Scripture calls "trouble of heart" are always future-related, vacillating between anxiety and hopelessness. Jesus spoke to his disciples' troubled hearts by promising them a place to stay with him, forever, in his Father's house: a true home.

A good place to stay will be a place where pain, grief, weariness, and fear are left behind, replaced by pleasure, anticipation, and satisfaction. It will be a place of *restoration*, where peace, purpose, and strength return and existence becomes worthwhile again. It will be a place of *revitalization*, where fresh energy for old and new tasks is found. The place Jesus promises will be all this and more.

What we often feel in ecstatic moments in this world—"I don't ever want this to stop"—will be the constant thought of our hearts in that world. We shall think it, knowing that in fact it never *will* stop.

Let our troubled hearts once latch on to this, and in the power of our faith we shall overcome the world.

J.I. Packer

Professor Emeritus
Regent College

Revelation 21:22–27

God's Everlasting Welcome

The first coming of Christ was humble, small, and offensive to human wisdom. I think we can all agree that his second coming should be more impressive. After Christ snatches us up into the sky, God's glory should be so overwhelming that we dissolve right into him, just like water droplets disappearing into the ocean …

But the author of Revelation 21 doesn't seem to see things this way. Here we find a paradox as mind-bending as the incarnation. The New Jerusalem is the dwelling place of God—and yet comes from God (21:11). It is dressed as a Bride—yet inhabited by the Groom. It is fully saturated by God's glory—yet replete with the marks of a redeemed humanity. The twelve gates are named for the twelve tribes. The twelve foundations are named for the twelve apostles. God's glory is everywhere, but the kings of the earth still bring their splendour into the city.

The New Jerusalem appears to be the union of the new heaven and the new earth—a union between humanity and divinity, Bride and Groom—so complete that the two become one.

Yes, the city is full of divine greatness, but it is also full of divine humility. The city comes *down* from heaven to earth. God comes *down* to make his dwelling place in the midst of creation. The New Jerusalem is the incarnation writ large across the universe.

> *He came down to earth from heaven*
> *Who is God and Lord of all.*

When I was a child, our nativity was shiny, clean, and ceramic. It sat on the grown-up dining room table far out of reach. We knew it was special because we were never allowed to touch it.

In the same way, we know that God is special because he is out of reach. In Revelation 21, it is fitting to see God and the Lamb on the throne, shiny and clean as they should be. We know the Lamb is holy because he's beaming with light. He's elevated and glorified—out of our reach.

But if we read more carefully, we see the story isn't so simple. There is a reason Jesus appears on the throne as a *lamb*. This is the same Lamb who was slain (5:12). This Lamb is not beyond our reach. In fact, he is so vulnerable that he bears the wounds of the cross for all eternity.

At the centre of the New Jerusalem is not a pristine, porcelain figurine. At the centre of all things is the God who has suffered for us out of inexhaustible love. This is how we know what is holy. The greatest difference between God and us is that he is love and we are not. Had we been the author, director, and protagonist of the drama, there's no way the story would have ended with blood on the throne. God's holiness is defined by his vulnerability. The Lamb's glory is defined by his love.

With the poor, the mean, and lowly
Lived on earth, our Saviour holy.

Matt Mattoon

PhD Student, Theology
Baylor University
Waco, Texas
Regent Alum (MCS 2008)

Luke 2:1–7

The Greatest Mystery

After Mary's song is recorded in Luke 1, the actual account of Jesus' birth in the next section seems almost an anticlimax. (Studying theology and living day-to-day often seem to have the same contrast!) The matter-of-fact data recorded by Luke seems, at first sight, to drag down the mystery of the incarnation into a sequence of facts, but the real story is about God entering the world he had created—not about how and when he did it.

Protestants may be judged to not sufficiently appreciate Mary, the icon of all disciples, as living out her obedience to the Word of God, as making Christ welcome, in the most amazing way possible. For this reason we need to accept "Mariology" as fruitful and inspiring study of the God-given role Mary accepted within the mystery of the incarnation. Various recent theologians, Italian and Spanish, have published books on the importance of personal experience as the most affirming way of approaching the Trinity and the mystery of the incarnation. And who but Mary experienced, more than any other human being, this mystery of God entering into our humanity?

On the other hand, the sober limitations of the biblical record are a check against the extravagance of Marian devotion often found in the Catholic Church. Karl Rahner suggests that the Catholic image of Mary reflects dominant cultural expectations about women. The historian Jaroslav Pelikan confirms this, having observed iconography about Christ through the centuries: Mary, a gentle mediator, with a harshly imperial exalted Christ; or, more recently (in a clerically repressive, anti-feminist culture), an idealized virgin. Central throughout iconography has been Mary as type and model of the church, so much so that Marian devotion has been deeply associated with the identity of the Catholic Church itself. But the idealism of Mary's submission to God, and of the feminine role of Mary within the Trinity, suggest anthropomorphic attempts to penetrate the profound mystery of God's advent in the humanity of Jesus Christ.

Our passage does not focus upon the moral merit of Mary, but rather upon the historical fulfillment of God's purposes with his people. Mary is surprised she is to become pregnant by "the power of the Most High." Yet this is the same God who called Abraham out of Ur, appeared to Moses at the burning bush, and whose Spirit led the prophet to select and anoint the shepherd lad David to become the new king of Israel. As God used the barrenness of Hannah, so we hear the echo of her song of thanksgiving in the Magnificat. Thus this narrative of the birth of Jesus is in a succession of previous divine interventions. Mary is not a solitary *Redemptoris Mater*. God has been preparing a place for himself throughout generations of those who have been willing to grant him room.

Joseph and Mary went to Bethlehem to register the birth of Jesus, "because he was descended from the house and family of David" (v. 4). In her appointed time, Mary gave birth to Jesus, in fulfillment of the divine word. Luke's emphasis demonstrates that the birth of Jesus, as descended from Adam, was that of a human being—a baby wrapped in swaddling clothes like any other human baby. Yet in his humble circumstances, "there was no place for them in the inn" (v. 7). So he was placed "in a manger." The Creator of the universe so embraced our humanity that he was birthed as a human being—into the impoverished circumstances of a peasant woman and her fiancé. God not only prepared this specific time and place for his entrance into humanity, but prepared for himself, throughout generations, a place of poverty and humility.

The overall impression left with us is the specificity of this historical event, its humility, and its complete "otherness," as the greatest mystery ever given to humanity. Is there "any room" for this mystery within our own lives?

> Oh Thou, whose glorious, yet contracted light,
> Wrapt in night's mantle, stole into a manger ....
> Furnish and deck my soul, that Thou may'st have
> A better lodging than a rack, or grave.
> ~ George Herbert, "Christmas."

Jim Houston

Professor Emeritus
Founding Principal
Regent College

LaVergne, TN USA
29 October 2010
202768LV00001B/2/P